MEMOIRS OF CHINA

William Craig

Hamilton Books
A member of
The Rowman & Littlefield Publishing Group
Lanham · Boulder · New York · Toronto · Oxford

Copyright © 2005 by
Hamilton Books
4501 Forbes Boulevard
Suite 200
Lanham, Maryland 20706
Hamilton Books Acquisitions Department (301) 459-3366

PO Box 317
Oxford
OX2 9RU, UK

Library of Congress Control Number: 2005930481
ISBN 0-7618-3324-2 (paperback : alk. ppr.)

Contents

Acknowledgments v

1 Going Prepared 1

2 Ready or Not 5

3 An Old Friend 7

4 The Students 11

5 The English Corner 13

6 Labor Day 17

7 Badaling 21

8 Serious Shopping 23

9 Being a Tourist 27

10 Getting Lost 31

11 Teaching the USA 33

12 The Old Neighborhoods 37

13 Arbor Day 41

14 Topsoil and Sand 45

15 Directly below Heaven 47

16 My Guides 51

17 Bob's School 55

18 Dragon Bone Hill 59

19 Like London? 61

Glossary 65

About the Author 67

Acknowledgments

I wish to thank Karen and my family for being willing to let me go to China and miss several months of snow shoveling and yard work. Likewise, I thank President Fagan, Roger Oden, and Larry Polselli at Governors State University for their encouragement and help in arranging my exchange. Thanks also to the staff, faculty, and students at China Youth University for Political Sciences for making a memorable trip into a wonderful experience.

1

Going Prepared

Like many Americans I have traveled around the country and have lived out of a suitcase for several weeks at a time. However, when I was approved to take a study leave from my university to teach at a Chinese university in Beijing, I began to think of what I needed to take for a five-month stay. From a mail-order house I bought a huge duffle bag with pockets and straps everywhere. Not only was it lightweight, but also it would hold an incredible amount of clothes and books. From our attic I dragged out my old three-suit rigid suitcase that my mother bought for me when I was going away to college. About a month before leaving, I began to practice packing my two large bags and two small carry-on knapsacks. After one practice run, I realized that I did not need to take a five-month supply of toothpaste and cotton swabs. I would take some and buy more later. I was going to a city of fourteen million people after all, not some small village.

I knew that one of the classes I was to teach at China Youth University (CYU) for Political Sciences was going to be an area studies course in American society and culture. I had found out about my courses two months ahead of time, so I was able to write a course book. A friend of mine word processed my notes into book form, and I had twenty-five copies duplicated. At this time, from things other people had told me, I thought that it might be difficult to have materials photocopied. In reality, the university had its own duplicating center, and there was an Office Max outlet down the street from the university on Third Ring Road. However, I was nervous about having enough workbooks for this one class, so I made space in my bags for the workbook copies.

My selection of books changed every few days. I knew that I would make use of every book I took, but which books would be the best? I wound up taking some histories; some novels (*House of the Seven Gables, Moby Dick, Little Women, The Red Badge of Courage, Manhattan Transfer, The Catcher in the Rye, The Natural*, and others); some writings (Thoreau, Mark Twain, John Rawls, and so on); assorted maps; copies of the U.S. Constitution; and news magazines and photographs from Chicago and University Park, Illinois (where

Governors State University is located), and from Rensselaer, Indiana (where we have lived for twenty-five years).

At least one of my new colleagues at CYU was an avid stamp collector, and because others would probably be interested in them, I bought sheets of commemorative stamps at the post office and some First Day Covers at Marshall Field's Department Store.

At the request of my wife, Karen, and my mother I bought a good set of long underwear for winter. Fortunately, or unfortunately, spring arrived in Beijing earlier than anyone could remember, just about one week after I arrived on February 21. I wore the long underwear only once when I visited the Great Wall at Badaling; there was still snow in the mountains and a brisk breeze.

I had an early morning Air Canada flight from O'Hare Airport when I left. So Karen and I drove to my daughter and son-in-law's home on the north side of Chicago to spend the night before the flight. After getting up in the middle of the night, we called for a taxi, got dressed, kissed my little sleeping grandson and headed off on the adventure.

My wife and I kissed goodbye at the airport—then I headed off on Air Canada for Vancouver. I had the good fortune of sitting next to a Chinese-American engineer who was on his way to visit a factory he owned outside Shanghai. He and I spent the four-hour flight to British Colombia talking about his impressions of present-day China. At Vancouver we wished each other well and went through Canadian customs. He had given me some great tips on things I might expect to find in Beijing, which I really appreciated.

The Air Canada flight to Beijing was full. It was the end of the Lunar New Year holiday (the Spring Festival), and people were heading back to China. Every seat in the plane was filled, but everyone was polite and, we were all well fed. Eleven hours is a long plane trip, but this day's trip was made about one hour longer by the arrival of President Bush to China. However, once we landed everything went very smoothly. I passed back a preprinted form at the China Immigration desk and showed my passport and visa at the customs counter. Three people were in the airport terminal with a sign to meet me. After introductions to Mr. Zhang (from the Foreign Affairs Office) and Tony Zhang and May Wang (both from the English Department), we went to the parking lot and headed off to China Youth University for Political Sciences.

I had purchased two maps of Beijing, so I had a reasonable idea about the expressways we were taking into the city that afternoon. If I had not seen a videotape a friend of mine had made for U.S. public television about Beijing, I would have been stunned by the traffic, tall modern buildings, and Los Angeles–style expressways I saw there. I was not naïve enough to think that I was going to see camel caravans coming to Beijing from the west. People who have not been to Beijing, or have not been back to Beijing in fifteen years, are in for a shock, though. The sea of bicycles has become a sea of taxis and private cars.

The Thursday I arrived in Beijing was a lovely winter day. It was warm. It was sunny. Things looked so very different. I tried to see everything on each side of the highway as well as carry on a reasonable conversation with my three hosts. It was very exciting being there. The four of us went out to dinner soon after arriving on the China Youth University campus. I remember having some great roast lamb, beef with peppers, fish, soup, and my first taste of Beijing beer (a German pilsner style). I had been in China for only five hours, but after dinner I was ready for bed. After the two plane flights and several sets of toasts during dinner, it did not take me long to fall asleep.

<u>2</u>

Ready or Not

I woke up thinking that this was my first full day in Asia, in China, in this huge city. My classes were not going to begin for a week—now was a great opportunity to get myself acclimated to my surroundings. I had brought a handful of coffee bags, so I had coffee before leaving my room for breakfast in the campus restaurant. When I went outside I could hear the traffic on Third Ring Road just outside the front gate of the university. It was seven o'clock, and the traffic was moving at a good pace. I later found out that the big traffic jams would happen an hour or two later in the morning. But now, cars, buses, and trucks were speeding along the twelve lanes, and birds were flying around campus. The students, staff, and faculty were not much in evidence. The Spring Festival vacation was ending, and many people were still traveling back to Beijing from their hometowns. It looked like a winter day; the sky was gray, it was fairly cold, and the canal next to the university was frozen.

Breakfast at the restaurant on campus was buffet style. I took some vegetables, some steamed bread, a hard-boiled egg, a dumpling filled with meat, and a bowl of porridge. I took too much. I had even imagined going back to the buffet table for another dumpling, but became too full to consider that.

This Friday was rather uneventful. I met with Professor Zhang and May Wang in the English Department office at ten o'clock and gave them copies of the workbook I had written and my friend Linda had word processed. Because one of my classes would be a large lecture course on American society and culture, we discussed the necessity of talking about religion. I let them know that I would not express my own religious views in class, just as I would not do at Governors State, either.

After lunch I started off toward a bank. One of my students in Illinois had exchanged 300 yuan (Renminbi [RMB]—"People's Money") with me for dollars, but I wanted to change several hundred more dollars into RMB. First, I left campus and walked to a branch of the Construction Bank of China. I went in and passed ten twenty-dollar bills to a young woman, who said she would exchange them for me. In a few seconds she slipped me two one-hundred-dollar bills through the tray. When I explained that I needed to exchange dollars into RMB, she, and one of her coworkers, explained to me that for dollars to RMB conversions, I needed to go to a branch of the Bank of China. They wrote out the address for me to give to a taxi driver, and I went back out on the street to hail a taxi.

There may be places in the world where it is just as easy to get a taxi as in Beijing, but it is hard for me to imagine such a place. Things went smoothly at the Bank of China—now I had 1,638 RMB instead of $200. My pocket bulging with 50 RMB notes, I left to find a return taxi. However, when I showed taxi drivers a card with the name and address of China Youth University for Political Sciences, I received puzzled looks. After having this happen several times, I pulled out a card from the Evergreen Hotel with the same address (because it was the conference hotel on campus). This worked. Evidently, the Evergreen Hotel has a large neon sign that the taxi drivers can see from the street. They recognize the hotel's name, but not the one for China Youth University (whose sign is not that visible from Third Ring Road). There was a standing joke among the students about always telling taxi drivers to go to the Evergreen Hotel.

3

An Old Friend

Saturday, February 23, was like a spring day in Beijing. After breakfast at the hotel restaurant, I left campus to go shopping. I wanted to buy some snacks, a few soft drinks, and generally see what the stores and markets in the surrounding streets had available. There is a pedestrian bridge across Third Ring Road, so I crossed it and headed off down the first small street or alleyway. Some small beauty shops, a newsstand, a noodle restaurant, and another beauty shop were on the right side of this street. A fruit stand, cigarette shop, small meat market, and another fruit stand were on the left side.

I walked three or four blocks down this very narrow street, avoiding being hit by any bicycles, taxis, or other cars. I saw several more tiny restaurants, a small grocery and household-goods store, and more cigarette shops and fruit stands. Now was the time to start buying. So, I picked four oranges at a fruit stand and settled on a price with the woman there. I was on my way to another shop when I recognized someone coming in my direction. Zhang Lei is a professor at China Youth University who had been at my university on an exchange four years earlier. I was very surprised to see him. Zhang Lei was not really surprised to see me because he had been trying to find where I was. One of the guards at the front gate had told him that I had gone across the road.

Zhang Lei suggested that he and I take the subway downtown to see some sights. Beijing's subways are fast, inexpensive, clean, and heavily traveled. They are not like Tokyo's, with people pushing, or being pushed, onto overcrowded subway cars. Still, Beijing's subways and buses get a lot of use. We got off at the station just under Tian'anmen Square and the southern entrance into the Palace Museum (the "Forbidden City"). Coming up steps from the station was a real spectacle: it was a warm late-winter morning, the sky was blue, and there were tens of thousands of people. It was an exciting scene.

If I had come to the square and Palace Museum by myself, I probably would have just stood there and stared for an hour. Both children and adults were flying kites over Tian'anmen Square. People were waving small flags they had bought from vendors. Large balloons with fringe were up in the air by the entrance to the Palace Museum; it was a really remarkable sight. However, I was not alone, and Zhang Lei had things he wanted to show me.

We went through the south gate of the Palace Museum to see the first courtyard. An array of people were looking around, buying tickets, and patronizing the souvenir vendors. Nine is the highest single number—so the huge doors entering the palace had nine rows of nine bolts each (to indicate the emperor, the highest of the "high").

It was too late in the day to begin a real expedition through the Palace Museum with its thousands of acres and hundreds of buildings. Consequently, Zhang Lei and I crossed the main street to Tian'anmen Square and walked its length. With the Great Hall of the People on the west side and the Museum of China History on the east, we walked south past Chairman Mao's mausoleum. People were selling and flying kites of all kinds. Other people were taking pictures or having their pictures taken. Some people looked as if they were Beijing residents out for a beautiful Saturday morning, whereas others looked like tourists (like me).

Zhang Lei had planned on going to the old Peking duck restaurant south of the square, Quanjude Kaoyadian. We were taken to a table on the upper level. The duck was wonderful, cut at the table into a pile of slices, each with a piece of crisp skin. Peking duck is served with a wrapper shell, chopped onion and cucumber, and plum sauce. This restaurant has been here more than one hundred years, and they certainly knew how to serve duck. We also had a shrimp and a beef dish, both of which tasted superb.

After lunch we took a taxi to Behai Park, northwest of the Palace Museum. There was a small admission fee (perhaps 5 RMB or 60¢). This may have been the first nice Saturday to go to a park, take a small rental boat out on the lake, or just go for a stroll. It would be two weeks before leaves started coming out on the trees, but many Beijingers were taking this opportunity to be outside.

Zhang Lei was really giving me an orientation to both Chinese culture and Beijing. This trip of ours was entertaining and instructive; the food was wonderful and of really significant cultural meaning. We walked about five kilometers that day, but we stayed at a slow pace so I could really observe things.

At Behai Park we saw some children's rides and games. The animal characters were not familiar to me, but they would be to anyone who was in China for very long. One was the Monkey King, perhaps the main character in Chinese opera/theater. He is very clever and outwits his opponents. He is very strong and is the only creature able to use his staff (which, being made from material from the bottom of the sea, is too heavy for others to lift). In mythology, the Monkey King is highly significant because he is the character who goes west with his friends to bring the Buddhist sutras to China.

It had been a full Saturday. By the time we returned to campus I was almost ready for bed. I did have dinner with Zhang Lei and Mr. Zhang, the gentleman from the Foreign Affairs Office whom I had met earlier, at the restaurant on campus. This dinner included roasted peanuts (which as an appetizer and because of its taste/texture difference during dinner is really tasty) and fish, roast lamb, and vegetables. The dinner, along with a number of bottles of Beijing beer, really prepared me for going to bed and sleeping soundly.

I planned to keep a journal of my trip and keep up with it every day. Now, after my second full day in China, I was going to put this off until the next morning. Over my five-month stay, I did keep up with the journal, but not always as dutifully as I had originally intended.

4

The Students

I had 261 third-year students registered for my lecture course in American society and culture. In addition, I had two classes of freshmen and sophomore students in oral English. Each of these two classes had about thirty-five students. Last, I had another oral English class for faculty members. This class met twice a week for two hours each day—late Wednesday and Friday afternoons. The faculty class started off with about forty participants, but ended with only about twenty-two attending semiregularly. Some teachers and professors had their own classes to attend at one or the other meeting times. All of them had conflicts at one time or another because they were giving tests, delivering lectures, or attending to some administrative details.

I had been told, on the first day I was on campus, of the importance China Youth University placed on this faculty class. All of these professors, lecturers, and staff members could read and write English well. However, the university reasoned that if they were going to be able to accept exchanges, attend academic conferences, and participate fully in discussions of their own disciplines, they needed more experience in speaking and listening to English. They were a dedicated and hard-working group. They had been teaching, reading, and writing all day long, and then they were giving up valuable free time at the end of the day (the start of the weekend on Fridays). There were several weeks at the beginning of the semester when most of these young men and women were rather reluctant to speak English in class. Two exceptions were a young man and young woman who were both professors of communications. They both had obviously worked at speaking English.

My university, Governors State University, is a suburban Chicago school that specializes in an older returning student population. Our average undergraduate student is about thirty-four years of age. At China Youth University, the students are generally in range of eighteen to twenty-three years of age. The faculty members I had for class probably averaged thirty-two years of age. Some of them had their doctorates; several of these were from foreign universities, including one from Heidelberg. I knew that they had all been excellent students as undergraduates. They would never have been admitted to college initially if they had not been. China simply does not have the money and resources to give places in college and graduate school to "late bloomers."

A graduate student in English from Beijing Normal University had been hired as my assistant for the term. Her name was Nina, and she planned to finish her degree in June and then become an English teacher at CYU in the fall. I met her the first afternoon of class. She was a very sharp young woman who must have decided to test me that day by asking, "Well, do you think this is exotic?" as we walked across campus to class. I was a bit startled, but realized she was partially joking. She may have been disappointed that I did not take the bait and say that I thought that everything I had seen in China was exotic. Nina, who was a lovely young woman, had to spend more time with her graduate thesis and so was with me only for the first half of the semester. She was a very big help at the start of a class with such a large group. I imagine that everyone believes, as I do, that she is going to be a great English teacher.

The students in my large lecture class were juniors from all the various majors at CYU. One young woman who attended with a friend was a finance major at People's University, a large university in Beijing. Sylvia was frequently the first student to come to class, so often we would have a chance to talk on a variety of topics with three other students who arrived early: two young men who were social security majors and a young woman majoring in law.

I had the opportunity to get to know a number of students in this lecture class well. It was a real pleasure not only to have them in class but also to go places with them in Beijing. They were a bright, articulate, hard-working group of young people, the majority of whom had a great grasp of English.

For this large lecture course I was assisted in taking attendance and photocopying sections of my workbook by a young faculty member from the English Department. May Wang was my main contact with the English Department and was a tremendous help in answering my many questions about what China Youth University expected of faculty members in their teaching, especially administrative details, such as when to make up classes missed during holiday times. As I am writing this book, May is taking linguistics courses at Marshall University in West Virginia.

5

The English Corner

It is difficult for me to limit what I tell you about my Monday-evening and Tuesday-evening English classes. The majority of the students were freshmen majoring in business areas. Monday's class also included a nine-year-old boy and a twelve-year-old girl. Their parents had probably told them to slip into class to practice English. The other students treated them like a younger brother and sister. They did participate fully in the class. The two younger students' English was very good, and they fit into the group rather well. The twelve-year-old did ask me at one point why middle school students in China had to study so much while, she surmised, that American students were having a good time and enjoying themselves. She was not convinced that the hard work would lead to getting into a good university and that American students had to do the same. She had probably just been given some big assignments at school and looked at me as though I had just told her the biggest lie ever. I have received the same look from students in the United States—it is nice to know twelve-year-olds worldwide know when they are being "put upon" by adults.

Students from my Monday night class took me with them to visit the old summer palace Yuanmingyuam. We also went as a group of seven, eight, or nine to the English corner at People's University. On Friday evenings this university has large numbers of people come to speak and listen to English. I went there for four consecutive Fridays in the very early spring, and even though it was cool and damp the crowds were large.

Before I went to this English corner, I assumed that several dozen students might come any particular evening. Alex, a junior law student in my large lecture class, went with me the first time. He had been there before and had a good idea that a huge group would surround me very quickly and that I would have a hard time moving about. He was correct. The site for this assemblage was around a fountain in a large garden area at the front of People's University campus. It was a lovely setting. Some park lamps lightly lit the area. As I looked around I saw that there were probably hundreds of people standing around in small groups of three to five people. We could hear people talking as we arrived, and Alex told me that he would meet me at a spot by the fountain in two hours.

In a matter of twenty seconds, I was completely surrounded by a cluster of very polite people who began to introduce themselves and ask cordial questions. How long have you been in China? What have you visited in Beijing? Where are you from? Do you like Chinese food? In about twenty minutes, approximately one hundred people surrounded me, and I felt as though I was lecturing rather than carrying on conversations. I began to ask certain people in the group questions in order to get them into a large discussion. Where are you from, Beijing? What should I see or do while I am here? Alex came back in two hours, and by this time I had a group of about 175 people around me.

I began to feel like a celebrity. The frightening aspect of all of this was that I was trying to answer questions for all of the United States. So, I had to keep qualifying my answers by saying "Many Americans feel this way on that subject, but many do not." Alex and I tried to leave after we had been there almost three hours. We moved about forty feet toward the edge of the park, and another group of people gathered around us asking questions. We finally excused ourselves and raced off toward the front gate of the university. Alex had bought me a bottle of water earlier because he knew I would need some after talking so much. We had been there more than four hours, and some people had stood talking with me for the whole time and had even moved with us as we tried to exit.

Alex managed to break his foot several days after we had gone to the English corner. His doctor did not want him moving around at all for about eight weeks, so it would be a while before Alex and I went anywhere. Because a group of my freshmen were interested in practicing their English, I suggested that this group of young women go with me to People's University on Friday.

It was probably much like traveling with a group of my own six granddaughters. These young women helped me on and off buses and made sure I did not step in puddles from the rain that day get hit crossing the main streets. Most of these students are hotel management and tourism majors. This was their chance to take a foreign visitor around Beijing.

They were very enthusiastic about visiting the English corner, and I thought that it was a great opportunity for them to practice conversational English. Unfortunately, this night (as on the other three nights I went to People's University), there were practically no foreigners or native English speakers in attendance. Tourists, visitors, and foreign residents do not seem to go to the English corners in any numbers. Around Beijing there are five or six well-known "corners", the one at People's University being the largest. In the four times I went, there were approximately two thousand people who came. Most people would talk with two or three other people. Blackboards had the locations of conversations on different topics in different places around this campus park. The attendees generally seemed to be in their twenties and thirties—about half were working people and half were students. Some people spoke almost perfect English, and others only listened. The second time I went, a French couple and I were the only foreigners out of the approximately two thousand to twenty-five hundred people attending; another time there was a Canadian and me.

One of the people who came the second night I had gone was a nine-year-old girl. After introductions, I asked her what she wanted to become after school was over. "A professor of economics" was her reply. "Are your parents professors?" "My grandfather is a professor of economics."

I then asked this girl if she came to the English corner often, and she said that she came every week to talk with her friends. I asked if these were boyfriends she was coming to meet—she laughed, and all the people around us laughed. Teenagers usually do not have boyfriends or girlfriends, let alone nine-year-olds. However, for young people in their twenties, the English corner is frequently used as a good place to meet members of the opposite sex. Students from one university can meet students from other universities, and people working in offices can meet others that they would not meet socially anywhere else. Likewise, it is in a very positive setting of learning. I hoped that I might be able to find a Chinese corner somewhere in Chicago where my grandson could learn Chinese.

One of the students with me met a young man that evening. He told her that he was twenty-three, and she did not believe it. So, when he asked her how old she was, she told him that she was twenty-five and out of college. Several of my junior students, however, had met their serious boyfriends or girlfriends at People's University on Friday nights.

<u>6</u>

Labor Day

At the end of the first week I was in Beijing, I bought a copy of *China Daily,* the English language newspaper, and found that the Lantern Festival was that evening. The newspaper story indicated that the setting off of fireworks was against the law in Beijing, even with the festival being that evening. Two supermarkets I walked by had long trestle tables set out in front on the street, and clerks were weighing and boxing small white candies. I thought that this must be a very traditional thing to buy and eat at the Lantern Festival and that I should probably buy a box. What I did not realize was that these candies had to be boiled before they were eaten. When they are cooked long enough, they are very tasty, but I might have popped a rock-hard one in my mouth. Luckily, I did not buy any because it seemed that the lines were too long to wait. I had some several weeks later, and they were really tasty.

I did see some lanterns being hung that afternoon and evening on campus. Some were added to the decorations still up from Christmas and the Spring Festival. However, just as I experienced in the United States on the Fourth of July, I could hear fireworks going off almost until midnight.

The big celebration that I did get involved with during my stay was for Labor Day, May 1. Several students played minor tricks on me in the spirit of April Fool's Day, but Labor Day was really a ten-day celebration. The Communist Youth League is the governing organization for China Youth University, and they were having a speech competition at the league's office near Tian'anmen Square. Someone at CYU had suggested that I might like to be invited and judge the contest because it was in English. It was interesting. However, even though they did tell me the scoring was from one to ten points, in tenths of a point, they did not say what might be the difference between a very good and an exceptional score. So, after the first of the eight contestants gave his introductory speech, I gave the young man a score of 8.5, thinking that was high for a good, but not excellent, introduction; then the scores of the other four judges came up—9.3, 9.4, 9.2, and 9.3. No one got another score that low that day from either me or another judge, although a few contestants did get an 8.8 or an 8.9.

The competition had three different categories: an introductory speech, a persuasive speech, and an exhibition of some talent. I have to admit that I may have added a few tenths of a point the next times I scored the young man I had initially given an 8.5. I did not want my initial score to denigrate his ability and total score. A faculty member from CYU in computer science was one of the eight contestants. His talent was to recite the value of *pi* to the one-hundredth decimal place. Probably because of nervousness, with about four hundred people attending, including some of his own students, he missed one number at about the sixtieth decimal place. He then missed several more numbers before finishing the last twenty perfectly. I told him later, in the taxi back to the university, that he should not have passed around a printout of all the numbers. Although it was very impressive, not a single person in that auditorium could have had any idea what the sequence of numbers was beyond 3.1416.

The Saturday before Labor Day, I was invited to a performance of the Beijing Symphony given for foreign teachers and experts working in the metropolitan area. It was held in a lovely new recital and ballet hall in the southeastern section of the city. Kevin, a young man from the Foreign Affairs Office, his wife (of two years), one of the university's drivers, and I went together. The performance was split evenly between western and traditional Chinese music, and it was exceptional. The four of us had a great time. It was the first time I had been to that section of Beijing and that part of Fourth Ring Road (the farthest beltway out in 2002).

The day before Labor Day, Mr. Zhang, Kevin's boss in the Foreign Affairs Office, met me in the student's dining hall and asked if I would like two tickets for another concert that evening. The young woman with whom I was having lunch at the time was taking a train to her hometown that afternoon, so she could not go. However, on the way back to my apartment from the dining hall, I met another of my students, and she was interested in going that night. The performance was by China's Military Orchestra in the recital hall at the National Library. This orchestra was, as American military bands are, probably made up of professional musicians who have military status. They played all traditional Chinese pieces, except for the encore, which was the "1812 Overture." Their performance was excellent and comparable to the Beijing Symphony's that I had heard three nights before.

I think the reason why I got tickets on the day of the performance was that, because many people were going out of town for the Labor Day holiday, some people had turned tickets back. I was glad to be able to go and happy some tickets were available. I wanted to buy a CD by the Military Orchestra, but although some people were selling tapes and CDs at the recital hall, there were not any by this orchestra.

Even though many people left Beijing for Labor Day, there were a lot of other people who came to Beijing. Because I could go to any of the historic sites on any weekend and even some weekdays, I decided not to go to places where there would be a lot of tourists. So, Lily, a student from Beijing Foreign Studies University whom I had met on the CYU campus, and I decided to go to one of the large shopping areas on May 1. Before the stores opened, we arrived at the Sedan Market. I wanted to buy a swimsuit, and when one of the large department stores opened, we headed for the sportswear department. I needed to try to find an XXL size, even though in the past three months I had lost several pounds and a few inches off my waist. The sportswear section was divided into small sections for different brands. At the third little area I found a pair of athletic shorts marked XXL, so I went to a fitting room to try them on. They were tight and truly uncomfortable, but I did not see other choices readily available. At another section of the store, I found another pair of swim trunks that were labeled XL but fit better than the others. I would have taken the first pair back, but the store was having a huge sale. The athletic shorts I bought first had been labeled at about 160 RMB or $21. The clerk gave me a discount, and I paid 105 RMB, and then we found out that we could turn in our sales receipts later and get back 60 RMB in coupons for every 100 RMB we spent.

That sounds like a great sale, does it not? Well, many people in Beijing thought so. Earlier, when the stores were just opening, it was easy to get around. From nine o'clock to ten o'clock we could browse around different parts of the first store and see everything. By eleven o'clock, however, the stores were packed. We were in the third department store, and it was so busy that at one place we had to turn around and make our way to another exit because the aisles were jammed. The area on the eighth floor to redeem store receipts into coupons had twenty young people working as cashiers, and each of them had two or three shoppers in line.

A parade was going on about twenty blocks east of this shopping district, and the Palace Museum and other tourist sites were having their biggest crowds of the year. However, in the Sedan Market, it looked like three or four football games had just ended. There were tens of thousands of people everywhere. The stores were filled, the little shops were filled, and the fast food restaurants were overflowing. Even with all the clamor, though, people were courteous and pleasant—perhaps partly because of the great bargains going on in the stores. Lily and I were able somehow to hail a taxi at lunchtime to find a quieter restaurant away from this shopping district.

The restaurant we found by taxi was still very busy at two o'clock in the afternoon. This place specialized in food from Hunan Province and was particularly delicious. We had grilled fish, along with a pork dish, little sweet-potato cakes, rice, and soup.

Labor Day evening I had a ticket to see the dress rehearsal for Beijing Television's Youth Day program. About twenty of my freshmen students were part of a large singing group from China Youth University that was performing in the program. Students from several grade schools and secondary schools, Young Pioneer (a political organization for children) groups, choruses from several other Beijing universities, and the People's Liberation Army were also going to be in this performance. This night was the dress rehearsal; the show was going to be taped the next night (Thursday) and then was going to be aired on one of the BTV channels on Youth Day (Saturday).

I met a group of seven of my freshmen students at the China Theater, which was just a block south of the university. They were all excited about seeing their classmates in the performance. We got some seats in the balcony because the main floor of this theater (seating for about twenty-two people) was to be used for the different music and singing groups. I have never been part of a television audience or rehearsal audience before, but there were long gaps in between segments, probably just as there are in American television. The producers checked applause levels, looked over the lighting, and cued the performers. The whole rehearsal took four hours for what would be a two-hour television program. We did get to hear the choral groups from our university.

The students were a bit disappointed that one movie actor and a television star scheduled to be in the show did not come to the rehearsal. I reminded them that we were lucky to get tickets for that night, because nonparticipant audience seats were so limited. It had been a busy day, and I was really tired at 10:00 p.m. when the rehearsal was over, but it had been truly memorable.

7

Badaling

After the first meeting of my lecture class, three students stayed and talked with me: Alex, Charles, and Emma. Alex was the young man who went with me to the English corner. Like Alex, Emma was also a third-year law student and a compatriot of his from Sichwan Province. Emma, a delightful young woman with great ability, was kind enough to go all over Beijing with me. Charles was also a third-year student, and he wanted to get a job as a tour guide. He told me that he would really like to take me to some historic sites and that I should just let him know when I would like to go. So, the next day when I saw him on campus, I told him I was ready to visit the Great Wall—how did Sunday sound to him?

I met Charles at six o'clock on Sunday morning. We took a city bus to the bus station at the Arrow Tower in north central Beijing. At least two ancient fortifications are referred to as the "Arrow Tower." One of these defensive strongpoints was at the southern end of Tien'anmen Square. The other one, the one we took the bus to, stood at a strategic place along the north edge of the old city wall, where Second Ring Road is now. I had also heard this arrow tower called the "Russia Gate." Now buses change passengers here for trips outside the city and other places around town. It was busy there on Sunday morning as we debated taking an ordinary city bus to Badaling for 7 RMB or a smaller, more comfortable bus for 10 RMB. We picked the more expensive bus (a 36¢ difference) and got on, and in a few minutes we were on our way to the Great Wall.

Badaling is about forty miles from Beijing and up about five thousand feet above the city. This bus did make a few stops to let more passengers on and off. In an hour we were past the last of the suburban sprawl and started the climb into the foothills. The temperature had been fairly warm in Beijing this week, considerably above normal for the last part of winter. However, even inside a full bus I could tell that the outside air was colder. We traveled the last twenty-five miles to Badaling were on an expressway that curved up into the mountains. Looking out the bus window, I began to see the remnants of several sections of the wall. It was difficult to believe that I was actually here looking at one of the world's most famous structures.

Badaling is very much a small tourist area. It is in a valley with mountain ridges rising up on either side of the gate in the wall. There is a museum of the Great Wall here, plus several small hotels, a number of restaurants, and a vast array of souvenir shops and open-air stalls. It had snowed in Badaling overnight, and people were cleaning the sidewalks from what looked like a five- or six-inch accumulation.

A lot of tourists were at this most popular section of the Great Wall on this day. The wind was cold, but the day was nice and sunny. Most of the tourists were from China, but there were some other Americans and some Europeans in little groups. From the gate and ticket window the wall climbs steeply up the hills on either side of this small valley. I had seen many pictures of the wall, but still did not realize the extreme angles that the wall is built on. I realized how out of shape I was as Charles and I went east from one guardhouse to the next. About five times as many people were climbing east as were climbing west of the ticket booth. When I took a look at the other section on our descent, I saw that the wall heading west was a much more rigorous climb to the first watch-tower.

It really surprised me how few western tourists were there that day. I guess I must have had the silly notion that, because the sections of the wall are so long (perhaps covering a length of 5,000 miles, with 3,000 miles of existing wall), people from China would be going to different sections. In reality, getting to Badaling and climbing this section is the most accessible for any tourist. My second silly notion was that Chinese tourists would not be buying the same souvenirs as Europeans. Of course, some tourists were not buying scarves, t-shirts, and plates decorated with the wall. Many were, however. My third notion, which perhaps was not so silly, was that the wall was built to carry horses, so it would be reasonably level. This certainly is not the case of this section of the wall. The incline between watchtowers at Badaling seemed in the thirty-degree range. I wondered whether the references to horses being used to patrol the wall meant mules. Charles did not have trouble with the climb, but for myself and others (I noted with a tiny bit of satisfaction) the ramp way and stairs were difficult. The view was worth the effort, though, with several thousand people climbing and descending directly below us.

Just stepping on the wall is a wonderful experience. I did see a number of tourists who never got farther than several hundred yards up the hillside and stopped there. It was also exciting just to see the Great Wall. And, even though the section at Badaling has been heavily rebuilt, it still left me with a feeling of the historical importance of this fortification.

8

Serious Shopping

The only hint of crime that I heard about in Beijing was the theft of bicycles. Most of my students had had at least one bike stolen, and several told me about losing three or four. Most of the students' bikes were black with very little chrome except for the handlebars. China Youth University had hundreds of bicycles that all looked the same, similar to other public bicycle lots, too. The students had their bikes stolen on campus, at other colleges, at shopping areas, and just about anywhere around Beijing.

There evidently was a location or two in our district of the city where people could buy bikes very reasonably (50 to 100 RMB). My students told me that the merchandise was probably the bikes that had just been stolen. The turnover in these bikes must have been huge, because many students told me that they had a bike for only several days to a week before it was stolen. I got angry about this situation a few times when my freshmen had their brand-new bikes, bikes their parents had bought, stolen. Because all of the students had locks on their bikes, and because the theft of them was so pervasive, I believed that an organized ring must be taking them.

The only time I believed I had been "taken" in a transaction was once when I bought an international phone card. I had gone to a small grocery store on the other side of Third Ring Road from the university instead of the branch office of the China Post (the official name of the China post office). At the post office a 100 RMB phone card cost 65 RMB—it was a standard discount. My mistake was handing the cashier a 100 RMB note without finding (or negotiating) the discount rate first. The cashier tucked the bill away and would not look up as I stood with my wallet open, waiting for change. This was really the only time during my six months in China that I had any trouble at a store.

In shopping at the department stores, all discounts were automatic. On some items the clerks would say there was a 10 percent, 25 percent, or 30 percent discount. For jewelry items there were usually deeper discounts of 40 percent to 50 percent. The Friendship Store had no discounts, but their prices were marked low anyway, and the quality of merchandise seemed much better overall than any other single store. Shopping in the Silk Market (near the Friendship Store in the embassy district), the Pearl Market, or in the Russian Market (for purses, luggage, or leather goods), I needed the help of one of my students to bargain with the sellers. At these markets the cash economy rules.

Emma, one of the students from my lecture class, went with me to the Pearl Market one Sunday. At one of the stalls I looked at a double strand of pearls for my wife. The clerk first quoted the price of 1,600 RMB (about $195), but said that I would get a discount if I bought both strands. Emma counteroffered 200 RMB, which caused a stunned look on the clerk's face. The clerk then offered to sell them for 800 RMB, to which Emma replied "200." We finalized this transaction at 280 RMB; we were pleased, and the clerk seemed moderately pleased.

I did go to the Russian Market by myself once. I had been in Beijing more than three months by this time and was feeling reasonably confident that I knew the value of items in RMB even if I was not an accomplished bargainer. Mornings are the time for the shops to sell wholesale items in quantity (evidently to Russian retailers), but it was late in the morning when I arrived. So, the shopkeepers quickly lost interest when I said I wanted to purchase just one of something. However, I did get one shopkeeper to sell me one huge nylon athletic bag (with "beijing" written on it) for 40 RMB. I thought that this had to be somewhat a fair price. It was about one-third of what I would have paid in Chicago at the very worst, and I liked it. Perhaps if I had been better at bargaining I could have gotten it for 30 or 35 RMB, but I bought it and much later crammed it full when I was preparing to return home.

Walking through this market with my "beijing" brand bag, I saw some purses I thought would make good presents back home. The clerk was willing to sell me one or two bags, although she was not too keen on the idea. They were stylish summer bags in a cotton weave; they would also pack fairly flat. The clerk gave me the price of 5 RMB. That sounded great until I checked my pockets and found only two one-yuan bills. The next higher amounts I had were 100 RMB bills, and the shopkeeper was emphatic about not making change. So I had to go back at another time to buy the bags as gifts, chiefly because I did not want to walk back to the nearest branch of the Bank of China and wait in line to get smaller denominations.

Some items, such as shaving cream and aftershave lotion, were not readily available in the numerous food markets and small stores. I think that most men in Beijing shaved with electric razors. Even large supermarkets did not carry shaving cream, and the stores that did have it carried American brands, which were more expensive than in the United States. However, I was within easy walking distance to shop for most things.

One small shop I frequently went into looked like a place you would find in Manhattan or Chicago's Loop. It was about five feet wide and was packed with everything from children's crayon sets to tennis racquets (things I did buy there). In this tiny little place, which could not have been more than 120 square feet of floor space, the young couple who ran it had lamps, tape players, clocks, radios, computer equipment, flashlights, soccer balls, tennis balls, ping pong equipment, envelopes and paper of every size, school supplies, gym bags, cameras, batteries, and desk organizers. This store probably even had shaving cream tucked away somewhere, but I did not ask about that.

The selection of audiotape players was large at some of the stores. I think most of the students had audiotape players for music and English pronunciation lessons. Videotapes were nonexistent because many people watched movies on their computers in DVD or CVD (compact video disc) formats. Practically none of the students had CD players, but they listened to CDs on their computer or their roommate's computer.

I went to see one movie while I was in Beijing—*The Lord of the Rings* dubbed in Chinese. Most of the students either downloaded movies off the Internet or traded DVDs. The movie theater I went to had a small lobby and ticket counter. The price was 50 RMB each for myself and Lily (the young woman who went with me). At the equivalent of $6 each, it was relatively expensive. The theater had a candy counter that sold bags of microwave popcorn, bags of potato chips, soft drinks, and candy bars. We were directed to walk two doorways east and go upstairs, because the theater had five or six movies playing and several of the theaters were in adjacent buildings.

The upstairs room we went to was about twenty-five by fifty feet, with about thirty living room chairs and small tables to put snacks on. The room also had a snack bar, which was open through the intermission. It was a very comfortable setting—almost like watching a movie at home. I had seen this movie in the United States three months earlier, but the young woman who went with me had not seen it before and was very excited about it. Lily liked the story so much that she later bought a set of *The Lord of the Rings* in English.

This was the only movie I went to see in a theater. I am sure there were larger theaters showing Chinese films. The one I went to was probably like an art theater in the United States that showed foreign films.

2

Being a Tourist

The third Sunday I was in Beijing I had made plans to go to the Summer Palace with Emma. We planned to meet at 8:00 a.m. at the front gate of the university. Not wishing to keep the young woman waiting for me, I arrived about ten minutes early. In the garden by the front gate about six students were standing by trees, practicing their English pronunciation. One of the students, a young man, came toward me, so I stopped, and we had a brief conversation. He wanted to talk with me to listen to English. We talked about how nice a day it was, how hard everyone was studying at the beginning of this new term, and how difficult it was to find a good place to practice pronunciation with five roommates. I had to excuse myself a few minutes later when Emma arrived from her dormitory, but I would see this young man about once a week and have little chats as we crossed paths on campus.

Emma is an exceptional student, majoring, as I mentioned earlier, in law. She had been an exchange student to Germany when she was in secondary school. And, although she had told me that she wanted to practice English listening and pronunciation, I was rather flattered that this young woman would be willing to give up a large amount of time guiding me about Beijing.

That Sunday morning we caught a bus just across the road from the university and took it to Peking University. Emma thought I should see this campus, and it was on our way to the Summer Palace. The campus was very quiet when we arrived, it still being early on a Sunday morning. It was a lovely university setting with lakes, a small stream, some artificial hills, and a temple. The campus and older buildings had been a prominent person's estate and mansions until late in the nineteenth century.

Emma had audited some classes at Peking University the year before and told me that although this was China's premier university, the student dormitories left a great deal to be desired. The classes she had sat in on, however, were great courses, and she had learned a lot in them. We had a nice chance to chat this warm winter morning. Emma, I found out, was an only child and had a cat, and her family had a garden. After seeing the sights of this impressive university, we decided to take a taxi to the Summer Palace and eat lunch.

Emma knew of an old established restaurant at the Summer Palace complex. The grounds of this Qing Dynasty palace included an artificial lake, an artificial mountain made from the digging of the lake, gardens, ancient cypress trees, and about one hundred buildings of various sizes. The regular restaurant served fast food, and evidently most of the foreign tourist groups ate there to save time. That day there was a wait for fast-food service, but we were ushered right into the regular restaurant to share a large round table with a middle-aged couple and their teenaged son. Emma ordered lunch of a chicken dish, a beef dish, soup, rice, and sweet cakes. This restaurant is rather famous because the recipes and chefs came from the training given by the chefs who worked for the last emperor. The food was very good, the service was excellent, and the total price for both of our lunches was $12 (no tipping, of course).

Meals at four- and five-star hotels in Beijing where foreign visitors stay are very, very good, expensive, and not authentic Chinese cuisine. Lunches at the Beijing Hilton or the Sheraton Great Wall will be in the $15 to $25 range (with tips usually added as a service charge). However, having the food is like having lunch at a Hilton or Sheraton in the United States, Europe, or South America.

Emma's admission fee to the Summer Palace was about half of mine. Students get discounts for movies and museums in China similar to those here; college students in China are on limited budgets, just as most American college students are. For many parks the student fee was 5 RMB, and at tourist sites it might be 50 RMB. These admission fees are, however, an extreme bargain. The Summer Palace is spectacular; the buildings are interesting, and the lake, manmade mountain, and trees are truly wonderful.

We probably walked more than seven or eight kilometers that day. It really felt like the first day of spring, too. In the morning the trees had no leaves, but in the warmth of the afternoon we could see the leaves opening the later it got.

By the time Emma and I had taken a dragon boat (a long, slender boat decorated with scales, wings, and a dragon's head at the prow) across the lake, walked around the islands on the far side, and walked back to the entrance, we were really tired. It had been a beautiful day, but I was glad to sit down in a taxi for the drive back to the university. Emma did not object to my suggestion that we stop for dinner at a Pizza Hut restaurant on our way back to campus. She and some of her friends had been there at least once before, and she really liked the salad bar. This brand-new Pizza Hut was built in an art deco style on the ground level of a thirty-story office building. I am more used to their suburban American venues, so the style was surprising. The menu was not at all surprising. It looked like Pizza Hut menus throughout the United States, but in Chinese, not English.

When I got back to my apartment and thought about how much walking I had done that day, I appreciated the new pair of walking shoes I had brought with me. I had ordered them from a sporting goods company's mail order catalog and had tried them on, but I had not worn them before leaving home. I had walked a lot (for me) this day, and it was a very good thing that the shoes were comfortable.

Believing I would have difficulty replacing my size 13 D shoes in China, I had actually packed two brand-new pairs in my luggage and worn a third. All three pairs were comfortable and had good gripping treads. I assumed that I would be doing a lot of walking in China, but I really had underestimated how steep the Great Wall is at places. I was truly happy that I had worn shoes that had not slipped on the steep ramps and steps at Badaling the Sunday before.

10

Getting Lost

Karen and I had bought each other guidebooks for Beijing, and I read the one for her before I left and took the other with me. Even though their evaluations of many things were similar, the guidebooks do not cover the same things. Charles, the young man who guided me up to the Great Wall, lent me a third tour book, which covered some parks and museums the other two had not. This is probably true of the different guides for any major city. Before this trip I had not been concerned enough, and was not staying long enough, in any major city to buy more than one guidebook.

Maps were another issue. I had bought two Beijing city maps at bookstores in the United States (one at the Complete Traveler in New York) and had also taken a large wall map of China. Charles and Nina had also each given me different Beijing maps. Now I had a rather good idea where things were. However, I frequently had to look at all four maps because some places or institutions (particularly universities) were only listed on one of the maps. One map had five or six universities shown, and another did not show any. But the only time I got turned around on directions was right on the China Youth University campus. Since this misdirection was rather humorous, I will write about it here.

Alex, the third-year student who had gone to the English corner with me the first time, had broken his ankle. He was told to stay off his feet, and so he stayed in his dormitory room in bed. I decided to take him some snacks and soft drinks, so I called him and got his room number—D 213. I was going bowling that afternoon with Kevin, the young man from the Foreign Affairs Office of the university. So Kevin and I went to the campus store and got Alex cookies, potato chips, candy bars, and several bottles of cola.

We walked over to the new dormitory, past the wing door marked "A," right to the last entranceway to the building. When Kevin and I walked in, there were two male students talking to a female guard. When Kevin said we were there to visit a student named Alex in a room on the second floor, the guard indicated that there was no one by that name there, and she walked away. We stood around in the lobby, and Kevin eventually asked to see a roster of the dormitory residents. Finally, after explaining that we were taking food to this young man with a broken foot, the guard went to get another young woman, who looked as though she was in charge of the dormitory. Shortly before this happened, I had thought to myself how very strange it was that a men's dormitory would have a young attractive female guard.

It would have been strange if it had been a men's dormitory. As has probably become apparent by now, of course it was not a men's dormitory at all. The guard was trying politely and subtly inferring that this was not a men's residence hall by saying, "You're in the wrong place." The other young woman had to be less subtle; she pointed across to another building, showing us the D wing. We were both doubly embarrassed: first, because we had not bothered to look at the sign that indicated the C wing and, second, because we were so slow in catching on to the hints we were amply given that we were definitely in the wrong place.

Kevin had been a student at China Youth University and then started working there for the Foreign Affairs Office. However, these dormitories had not yet been built when he was a student there. So, we did finally get to Alex's room, tried to cheer him up with the snacks, and then went off campus still feeling just a little foolish.

11

Teaching the USA

Before anyone gets the idea that my stay in China was all just enjoying myself by visiting tourist sites and eating wonderful meals, I need to mention something about my work at CYU. I usually spent at least two hours of preparation for each hour I had of class. Because I had twelve hours of class a week, I really needed to spend an additional twenty-four hours getting ready for them. I had made a workbook for my American society and culture class, but I needed to make up vocabulary exercises and other worksheets and English usage games for my other four class meetings. The games were intended to encourage discussion, and I started off the first set of classes talking about baseball as a way of getting them used to hearing me speak. I had brought stacks of baseball trading cards and had the students introduce each other to the players on their cards—which team they played for and in what city. I showed American League cities and National League cities on a large U.S. map. I drew a baseball field on the blackboard and showed the difference between hits, fly balls, and fouls. After two weeks it was easier for the students to understand my accent and voice.

My main teaching goal was to improve the listening and speaking skills of these classes of students and faculty. So, after the baseball references, we began to talk about introductions and identifying ourselves—where we were from and information about our families, our academic interests or college majors, hobbies, and entertainment interests. One booklet I took with me had floor plans of historic homes from Sturbridge Village, the reproduced New England village west of Boston. In the faculty class these created a lot of discussion. The idea of having a house built to someone's own specifications was much more than just slightly interesting to the teachers. A few new single-family houses were being built in Beijing, but they looked as though they would be outrageously expensive. In the suburbs there was building going on—very little of it for single family homes, but there was some.

In the faculty class we must have talked about apartments and what their dream homes would be like for at least twelve hours. The majority of married teachers had much less space, for a family of two or three, than I had for just myself. I think that my apartment had about four hundred square feet, including the bathroom. The single faculty usually shared an oversized dormitory room. But everyone was interested in the possibility of having a garden of his or her own—maybe more than extra living space. Hardware stores, much less large home-remodeling stores, were not in evidence in Beijing. Wal-Mart had announced that they were going to build a number of stores in major cities, and they will certainly carry hardware. However, most faculty did not have a good idea where they could buy plywood, plasterboard/sheetrock, 2 by 4s, and so on. Many furniture stores sold bookcases and other wall units that required assembly, but there were not places with supplies for remodeling.

Some of the teachers were in the process of buying an apartment; others had not saved enough money or were skeptical about taking a large mortgage for an apartment. Only one of my faculty students was an economics professor. He, of course, was very familiar with interest rates, financing, and investments. So, one of the topics we discussed at length was investments. The economics professor did have some stocks from either the Shanghai or the Hong Kong exchanges, and others had wondered about stocks, bonds, and the new option (in China) of mutual funds. We discussed the different merits of particular investments and then, as practice, selected some stocks and tracked them. Because the two Chinese markets were as volatile as those in the United States and Europe at the time, people became nervous with our pretend investments losing pretend money.

We checked the stock prices at the start of class each Wednesday and Friday afternoon. On one particular Wednesday the stocks we were tracking had lost more than 10 percent of their value. As nervous as the students appeared to be about our test investments, I do not think I convinced anyone that investing one's money in stocks was a good idea just then. I had to admit that at this particular time stock markets looked more like gambling than investing. Added to this was the fact that no one in this class knew much of anything about the companies whose stock was being offered.

We did discuss a book that had just been written by a Boston University sociologist titled *One Nation, After All*. This study pointed out the finding that, even though there is a disparity in wealth, jobs, and empowerment in America, on critical and basic values Americans have a surprisingly high agreement (sometimes agreement is at the 90 to 95 percent level). This study disputed the media (both American and Chinese) that portrays Americas a divided society.

Because almost all Americans describe themselves as being middle-class, in the faculty course we discussed the difference between what Americans would categorize as "middle-class morality" and what Karl Marx believed about the nature of the "bourgeoisie." We talked about their situations; would that sociologist classify Chinese university professors as "middle-class?" I think some of the faculty members had not really thought about making distinctions between being middle-class and being part of the "bourgeoisie."

My Thursday evening course in American society and culture also discussed that sociology book. The students in this course generally had the impression that because America was so diverse ethnically, it then must be very divided in its basic values. Several of the students were very interested in this study, and I left my copy of the book for them. The two topics I covered with this class that seemed to draw the most questions were my daughters' weddings and the vacation trips that my wife and I had taken recently. Because these Thursday students were, I imagine, all about age twenty or twenty-one, they were interested in travel and marriage. They wanted to know where and when my daughters had met their husbands, where they had gone on dates, and where they had gone on their honeymoons. Students also showed a lot of interest in our national parks. I talked about walking trails at Glacier Park and Isle Royale and seeing moose, elk, and bear. The idea of being in a wilderness area with so few people, and with or without large wild animals, was fascinating to them. There are similar wilderness parks in China, but they are difficult and expensive to get to.

Teaching at China Youth University was, as I hope I have made clear, was an enjoyable and memorable experience. I sincerely hope that my students gained a lot from my courses. I certainly gained a great deal from the students.

12

The Old Neighborhoods

On my fourth Sunday in Beijing, Emma and I planned a trip to visit the old neighborhoods in the north-central part of the city, just south of Second Ring Road. We took a cab to a main street just north of the Forbidden City and walked past a long row of pedicabs waiting to show tourists the sites here. Emma thought that it would be much better to deal with an individual guide, and one did come forward to offer his services. We agreed on a price for a two and one-half hour trip. On a standard plastic map he showed us which sites he would take us to, but he was not part of the row of licensed pedicabs that all had the same signs and uniforms.

Our guide then went off to his (or perhaps a rented or shared) pedicab for what would turn out to be more than a four-hour trip. I thought it was a good thing that Emma was slender and light because of all my extra weight on this tricycle cab. I thought this even before our driver and guide said it jokingly to Emma in Chinese. Later, I guessed that the driver spoke no English, so he could not work for the tourist company. We were getting a deal because Emma could interpret fully, not just because she was good at bargaining and knew the value of things. We had his services for an extra ninety minutes or so because he liked us. He even introduced us to other drivers. I think he was pleased to be guiding a beautiful student and her teacher around. Emma had not been to this neighborhood either, so we were both very interested in everything we saw.

We first took some narrow alleyways (*hutongs*) that were only two pedicabs wide. He showed us how the houses were arranged in different ways inside the street entrance. He had a route and stopped at homes of people he knew. We saw rooms, kitchens, shared open spaces, and little gardens. It was morning and still cold, so some people had wooden stoves burning to take the chill out of the house. Our guide showed us the differences between the size of doorways and front steps that indicated greater wealth. He showed us the difference between Ming Dynasty and Qing Dynasty decorations on the steps.

I will not list here all of the names of places we went that day. I am sure that most guidebooks list what is seen in a standard tour of this section of the city.

We did visit an active Buddhist temple, a palace that once belonged to the last emperor's (Pu Yi) father, the former home of the playwright Guro Mauro, and the home of the woman named "honorary president of China," Song Qing Ling. It is evident at her former residence, now a museum, that she really loved children. Her library is one of the most comfortable-looking rooms I have ever seen. I visited her home twice more, once with two of my freshmen students and again when Karen and my daughter Cara came from the United States.

It was past the lunch hour by the time we finished our tour. Our guide had really added sites we had not expected when we struck the bargain. At the end, Emma told me that the guides usually did get a tip. He left us at the Silver Ingot Bridge at a pretty spot dividing two sections of a lake. Pointing out a barbeque restaurant for lunch, he showed us how we would walk over to the Drum Tower from this bridge.

The Drum Tower is about 750 years old and stands guard at the north end of a market street that divides Beijing east and west. At the entrance is a large gift shop that sells art and jewelry items from Tibet. A long divided staircase took us up about five floor levels to the observation deck and drum room. A group of music students was putting on a demonstration of beating these drums at 2:30 p.m., and we climbed to the drum room just a few minutes before it started. Most of the drums used in this demonstration were about six feet across. I wondered when I heard this whether the sound could carry all the way to the Palace Museum, about two miles directly south.

About two hundred yards north of the Drum Tower was the Bell Tower, built about 150 years earlier. What appeared to be the largest bell on the planet hung above a deck, again about five stories up. When Emma and I bought admission tickets, we went to the entrance and looked up at this second staircase; I think that both of us wondered whether we really wanted to climb another set of stairs that day. However, we did go up. The bell was gigantic, and I could not imagine how it could have been lifted and put in place.

When we finally climbed back down from the deck of the Bell Tower, my legs felt as though I was on a ship in heavy seas. I wobbled out to the street and suggested that we take a cab to the Friendship Hotel and eat at the T.G.I. Friday's restaurant there. It was near campus, and I was sure that if Emma liked McDonald's hamburgers, then she would like some of the meals here. I had been dropped off by a taxi there my fifth day in Beijing and had stopped for a late lunch. The restaurant this Sunday evening was very quiet. There were people at only three or four other tables when we came in, and it was nice in a quiet atmosphere to sit down, relax, and have hamburgers and lemonades. Even with rides in taxis and pedicabs today, we had walked about five miles before dinner and were about to walk another two miles back to the university. I reminded myself on the walk back not to complain about my aching feet tomorrow morning to Karen when I called home to Indiana. I was positive she would not be sympathetic to any whining from me, because there had been a snowstorm raging in the Chicago area, and no one had forced me to go sightseeing with a pretty twenty-one-year old student. I was correct. The next morning when I phoned home she did not want to hear me complaining about sore feet. I talked about the great view from the Drum Tower.

13

Arbor Day

I ate about four lunches in a week in the faculty and staff dining room. This room was open for breakfast and lunch every weekday, and I ate there partly for the convenience, partly to see people, and partly for the food. I really enjoyed the noodles, dumplings, and most of the other basic lunch dishes they had. I sometimes would eat with some of the faculty who were in my class, one man from the Economic Development Office, Mr. Zhang from the Foreign Affairs Office, or one young man from the Physical Education Department. Usually, however, I had lunch with three young people from the computer office, Kevin, and four young faculty women. Two of these young teachers were Amber and Isabelle from the English Department. They were about my daughter's ages and had just finished their master's degrees at other universities. They both had boyfriends who came to visit them during holidays, and each had plans to get married. We had some very good conversations, and it was a pleasure to be introduced to their young men.

I would also often have lunch with two other young women; one did publications for the university, and the other was a professor of psychology. They had been at CYU for their undergraduate degrees one year apart, and they were members of the faculty mountain-climbing club. Kevin and his wife and a young journalism instructor with the English-sounding name "Lincoln" were also members of this club. They had planned a day-long set of activities, beginning with helping to plant trees in a reforestation area, for a Saturday in early April, and they invited me to join them. So, a day or two before this trip, I went to the campus store to buy a canteen kit. I bought a plastic one with two deep dishes and a locking lid that had a compartment for a spoon and chopsticks. I packed two small bottles of water, my camera, and some granola bars. I was all set for the trip.

I had offered my apartment on Saturday to two of my junior students, Frank and Judy, to have a birthday party with their friends. They were very excited to have a real kitchen to cook in and a dining room table to sit around. Most of the students had some electric pots in their rooms to cook with, but there were not any kitchens in the dormitories or any rooms to have a party privately. So I gave Frank and Judy my apartment key on Friday night, and the next morning I carefully made sure I had everything I needed for the trip and then locked the door.

We were supposed to meet at the front gate at 6:00 a.m., and I was the second person there. We had a small bus that seated twenty to take us out into the country. There wound up being more than twenty of us going on the trip, so someone went to get a car, and four people went in it. The trip to the mountains went out past the Summer Palace toward the northwest. We were going to start at a tree farm in the foothills. It warmed up considerably in the ninety minutes it took us to get to the farm.

A large farm truck met us at the field, which was piled high with saplings that were about eight to nine feet high and about four inches around the trunk. The trees had been in another field planted about eighteen inches apart, and we were going to plant them in double that space. These trees were a hybrid variety from Korea that was particularly drought resistant. They will be moved one more time before they are planted permanently.

We had 350 trees to plant, but fortunately holes had been dug and filled with water the day before. So, we only needed to do the positioning, refill the holes, and make sure that the soil was filling in around the roots. In teams of two we planted the trees in about three hours. We then went to lunch at the tree farm's greenhouse and warehouse area. The saplings we planted had started off in these greenhouses about three years before.

One member of the club had made noodles early that morning and cooked them over an open fire for our lunch. They were really good, especially with the several different types of mushrooms. We were all ready to eat when he was ready to serve. Several people commented on how nice my plastic bowl set was and wondered whether I had brought it from the United States. I told them it was "from the campus store—12 RMB." We had a number of cases of Beijing brand beer, and a couple of the men brought what probably were some expensive bottles of rice wine. Everything was very informal; some people had brought other food items to share, such as vegetables and rice wine (that tasted like 100 proof). It was all very good, and I was certainly ready to eat lunch.

We finished eating, cleaned everything up, got in our bus and car, and started off to the park at Phoenix Peak. Because we were already in the foothills, it was not a long drive to get into the park. Phoenix Peak is about 6,500 feet in altitude, and we had a fifteen-minute climb in the bus up to a parking lot at the trailhead that was probably at about 3,500 feet. About two hundred other hikers and climbers were there that Saturday. I did not see any regular city buses there at all, just a few taxis and a few small buses like ours; the rest were private cars and one very sporty-looking black motorcycle.

It was nice and warm up on the mountain. The air was very clear; however, looking east-southeast we could see some haze over what were the suburbs of Beijing. The two species of birds that I had been seeing all spring were there at the park, along with a variety of smaller birds. The two types of birds I was interested in were both black and white: one had a long tail like a flycatcher, and the other had a red head and looked like a magpie. I am sure they are both common in north China, from what students told me. From its distinctive call, the magpie-like one is nicknamed "the happy bird." Someday soon I will need to stop at the Brookfield Zoo in Chicago to see whether they have a bird guide to China.

The trail up this part of the mountains was wide and followed a streambed for about two-thirds of a mile. Then there was a small flat area where a temple had stood. From that area the trail went up a rock cliff face with toeholds cut in the rock and a cable to pull oneself up. I took a look at this climb and decided that I had better not go any farther. I am not at all agile and believed that I would not be able to function at CYU if I sprained or broke an ankle. So, I took pictures of everyone else going up, enjoyed the sun a little longer, and then hiked down to the parking lot area.

About six people in our group had not started the climb at all, but instead were playing cards at a concession stand that sold snacks, Coke, and beer. After tree planting and a bit of a hike, I did not feel guilty about sitting in the shade, drinking beer, and playing rummy. All six men were friendly, but not overly or "forced" friendly, and our conversation was really limited because they did not speak English, and I did not speak Chinese. By using hand signs they found out that I was fifty-seven, and I found out that one of them was fifty-two. Someone later told me that most of these men were part of the security force for the university. I recognized many of the young men who were uniformed guards at the university and frequently had conversation with one who was teaching himself English. Now I had also met most of the regular security force of officers. Thinking about it later, I would say that was the safest I had ever been anywhere before.

The faculty mountain-climbing club had planned another excursion for later May or early June. However, even though I had looked forward to going along with them, I probably needed to be just as cautious as the trip in April. I had not gotten more agile, and spraining or breaking an ankle in May would have been just as problematic.

14

Topsoil and Sand

In mid-March the wind storms started. People referred to them as dust storms. However, they really are sand from the west and topsoil from the north being blown into Beijing by two different wind patterns. I remember almost exactly when I saw them. One Thursday evening after my lecture class, four students (Emma, Alex, Judy, and Frank) and I went to the Tibet Bar for what is called "strawberry tea." Strawberry tea is made with crushed fresh strawberries, water, and sugar, and it tasted like a milkshake. Lemon tea, I assumed, was much like a lemon shake. This bar was just outside one of the gates at the Central Minorities University, about four blocks down an old alley barely wide enough for two small cars to squeeze past each other. By walking very close to the edge of the pavement and watching for cars and vans constantly, we were able to get to the bar safely. In the two hours we were there we talked about my impressions of China and their impressions about the United States. These were four of the brightest students I have ever been around. The past Thursday, Emma, Alex, Charles, and I had talked about the upcoming World Cup matches. This week we were talking about everything.

The Tibet Bar was a fascinating little establishment. It was a tiny brick building with a small door, a small window, and a tiny wooden sign that could be very easily missed. They had beer and a Tibetan grape wine (which Emma said was very good), and a huge variety of teas, leaf and fresh fruit. The place had two rooms. One was a cozy room with a wooden block floor, wooden beams, a fireplace, bookshelves with books about Tibet, and six tables with chairs. The other room had a tiny bar with glasses and bottles, a couple of stools, and some extra beer crates. The public toilet was out the back door (the WC for this neighborhood).

When we left to go back to CYU, we had to share the alley with any number of small diesel tractors in both directions that were pulling carts. By a city ordinance these tractors and many trucks are kept off Beijing streets until after 9:00 p.m. or so. Now they were out in the little roads in force, and we really had to watch where we stood or walked. Added to this, the sand and topsoil storms had begun. The wind seemed to be blowing directly at us, and the tractors, combined with their noise and fumes, made for a difficult hike back. All of us were trying not to breathe deeply.

The students had told me that the dust storms would last for three or four weeks and that I had better keep my windows and balcony door closed to keep the dust out. However, most of the time you could not tell when the wind would pick up, and my apartment was very warm because the steam heat was still on. The next day, right after my faculty class, I met Wu Qing and his assistant for dinner. Wu Qing was in charge of the Economic Development Office at CYU, and he had asked me to give a lecture to interested students on Friday night on graduate education in the United States. I met them in the lobby of the new teaching building, and we went to dinner at a restaurant on campus. His assistant, a young woman who was a senior student intern, ordered a banquet for the three of us: fish, roast lamb, tofu, a shrimp soup, and chicken with vegetables. I tried not to get stuffed, but it was difficult not to overeat.

After dinner we went back to a lecture hall at the teaching building for the program. Ten minutes before the program began, the room was filled. The hall looked like it was meant to hold about 250 students. By the time it was to start, about thirty students were standing at the back, and another fifty were outside in the hallway. I talked for about an hour, had questions for another hour, and then finished with another fifteen minutes of conversation with students on our way out of the classroom. My thirty years of college admissions work helped me explain what things ought to be included in a student's personal application statement and why students should explain their reasons for applying to a particular graduate school.

After the questions were answered, the student intern walked me back to my apartment building. As my host for the program, she did an excellent job, and I thanked her for preparing everything so well. As we were walking the short distance to my side of the campus, I should have been paying more attention to the wind. It was blowing a little bit, but after I returned to my apartment the wind got even stronger. If I had been paying attention, I might have shut my windows and balcony door. However, I was really tired, and it seemed nice to have the breeze coming in. The next morning, though, I saw that the breeze had brought a sand-and-topsoil covering to my floor, desk, table, everywhere. It took me several hours of sweeping and washing to get my room cleaned up again, and I became much more careful about leaving the windows and door open.

15

Directly below Heaven

Two of the loveliest buildings in Beijing are at Tiantan Park, southeast of the Forbidden City/Palace Museum. The Temple of Heaven and the Temple of Prayer were where the emperors went to pray for good harvests. Both buildings are circular, with deep blue tile roofs. The buildings at other sites (the Summer Palace and the Palace Museum, among other historic sites) were all rectangular, except for a round building at the Imperial College, the site where the highest-scoring test-takers on the civil service examinations studied. Tiantan Park is really a lovely place. Acres of ancient cypress trees, flower beds, raised walkways, plus these beautiful buildings make it really spectacular.

My student friend Emma and I went here in early April on a Sunday morning. Outside the front gates an elderly man with water and a very large brush practiced calligraphy on the pavement. In one movement he was drawing these complex characters without lifting his brush. Emma explained to me that those were the old-style characters still used in Hong Kong and Taiwan (the People's Republic moved to a simplified character style in the 1950s). We stood and watched him for ten or fifteen minutes. It was really fascinating watching this man write so smoothly, almost effortlessly.

Emma told me that he was writing a poem, but she could not read or draw the old characters. One of my faculty students was very interested in calligraphy, and everyone appreciated the beauty of the older style. However, few of the younger people could read past one or two lines of characters.

When my wife and older daughter, Cara, came to visit me in May, the Temple of Heaven was one of the sites I put on a "must go to" list. On the day that Emma and I went, the windstorms were still a problem. The Circular Altar, where crop sacrifices were made by the emperor, was a raised stone platform high enough up to catch the full impact of the winds that were blowing more than thirty miles an hour that morning. We did not stay long up at the raised altar, even though no sand or topsoil accompanied the wind.

Because of the high winds there were not any clouds in the sky that day, and the sky matched the deep blue tile roofs of the park's buildings. Emma and I left there about noon, and we decided to go to the shopping district for lunch and to look around. Emma said that she and her friends usually went shopping on either Saturday or Sunday. Most of the time was spent just looking and seeing what was available. We took a taxi to the fanciest of the indoor shopping malls and ate at a place that was decorated like a rainforest, complete with fish aquariums, artificial foliage, and the sounds of rain and thunder.

This shopping mall had stores from Milan, Paris, Tokyo, and New York. They could have been in any major city and probably are in Shanghai as well as Beijing. Several of the stores, though, did have very nice things that were unique just to Beijing, and I did buy a couple of items to take back home for people: a large silk scarf and a light silk blouse.

Emma's favorite store was there. It was part of a Chinese chain of stores selling clothes to college-age women. The items they carried looked both somewhat modern and somewhat traditional, and they were in whites and pastels for summer. They reminded me of prints I had seen at a Laura Ashley store in Indianapolis where one of my daughters had picked out bridesmaids' dresses.

We then went to another large department store nearby where I almost bought my little grandson, Alvin, a child's violin for 800 RMB. There was an instrument-making shop in the basement, and I did look at them for a long time. Emma thought that I could always come back and buy one. She sounded just like my daughters did when they thought that I should wait and talk the purchase over with my wife. I did, however, have grandchildren on my mind because Anne, my other daughter, and Wade, her husband, had just taken three-day-old Brianna home from the hospital the week before. Still, I did not buy Alvin the violin then and did not have anyone asking me why I had bought a twenty-month-old boy a violin.

Emma and I suddenly realized that we needed to get back to campus to meet Frank and Judy for dinner. We went outside, hailed a taxi, and went about half a block before being stopped by a policeman. Our taxi driver had picked us up too close to the intersection and got a ticket. It was already time to meet Judy and Frank, and we did consider getting out of the one taxi and getting into another that could get us moving. But we felt guilty about leaving the taxi driver with no fare and a stiff fine. We waited, and the driver came back from the police with his citation in hand. When we got back to the university, I gave him some money to help pay the fine that we felt somewhat responsible for.

Judy and Frank were waiting patiently for us to arrive back on campus. We apologized, adding that my pocket watch had run down several hours before. We did think that it was much earlier. We walked across the pedestrian bridge over Third Ring Road to hail another taxi to take us to dinner. I carefully walked well past the intersection to put my arm out for a taxi, not wanting to get another driver a ticket. I suggested taking the students to T.G.I. Friday's, and Emma agreed that it would be a good place. They liked going to McDonald's, and this would be a different experience with different burgers and desserts.

Because I was positive the students would not ever go back to the Friendship Hotel and Friday's, I thought that we should walk around after dinner. This older hotel complex is huge, so we walked around and looked at the gardens and the small floodlit golf driving range. I had to explain what it was used for without having a golfer hitting balls there to give a visual demonstration.

Sundays were usually such perfect days of sightseeing that I looked forward to them. But I enjoyed seeing my students so much on weekdays that I did not mind Monday mornings and preparing for classes. I had no Sunday evening or Monday morning blues.

16

My Guides

On April 1, "April Fool's Day," I received a call from one of my students in the morning saying that she and two of her classmates were coming over to my apartment to talk. After I had agreed and hung up the phone, I started to think that this was strange. In about a half hour Song Xia, Charlotte, and Vivian arrived looking very sheepish. What they had planned on was to call me, and when I said "no, don't come," they would say "April Fool's" and invite me to lunch at the student dining hall. When I said it was all right to come, they had to change plans. We did go to lunch and then had a nice two-hour talk and walk along the canal. It was a great spring day—just the right temperature.

These three young women were part of a group of about ten young women who were all in my Monday evening class for freshmen. These were the young women who went to the English corner on Friday nights with me, and later in the term we would frequently eat dinner together before class. They were all about nineteen years old, and practically all of them were in a hotel and tourism management program. They were really a delightful group of young people.

One evening after class these students told me about their class trip to the Great Wall. They had gone there a few weeks after I had been there. I began including in our class conversations discussions about the merits of various tourist and historic sites. One place several students had been to and others wanted to go to was Yuanmingyuan—the ruins of the Old Summer Palace. In the 1840s and 1850s Europeans had described this as one of the loveliest places on earth. The palaces were built in a unique style to incorporate Chinese and European Renaissance architecture in a setting like Versailles. In the 1860s an Anglo-French army destroyed the palace, and in 1900 U.S. marines and troops from Japan, Russia, and other European countries came and burned what was left standing.

So we decided in class that we would go to Yuanmingyuan on a particular Saturday. I got to our meeting place first and was first joined by three others and then two more shortly afterward. The six of us waited and waited. Finally, two people were sent back to the dormitory to find the three students whom we were missing. We crossed the road, waiting again for the others at a large bus stop. Eventually, the others showed up, except for one young man who was from another university. After considerable debate about which bus to take we literally jumped on one going our direction that looked as though eight of us could find space. The bus let us off about half a mile from one of the entrances, so off we went and bought tickets. When you look at this park on a map of Beijing, it is a large green area, not particularly well marked, to the north and east of the Summer Palace. I went there twice, once on this Saturday with my students and again on a Sunday with Emma, Karen, and my daughter Cara—this second time on a warmer May day, however.

When I went with the students we walked the three miles of trails back to the palace ruins. We stopped and ate the food that each of us had packed for the day. We had quite an assemblage of food with us. I was ready to eat, too, when we stopped for lunch. I had also brought cleaning wipes, soap, napkins, a knife, and some plastic spoons that I did not think the students would bring. The oranges I brought were a hit, but the granola trail bars were not.

We took a lot of pictures on this trip. The buildings must have been spectacular before the destruction because the stone-carved building blocks were so original and ornate. Sometimes it seemed as though we had this whole park to ourselves. There were really not many people here either time I visited. It is not mentioned in many guide books, so tourists do not go here in the vast numbers they do to the "new" Summer Palace. A great deal more walking is involved unless you take the shuttle bus, as we did when my wife and daughter came. The day I was there with my students I felt as though I must have walked between seven or eight miles. I took two rolls of film because the students wanted to pose or take pictures everywhere. We took pictures of us standing on lovely curved bridges, by the stone ruins, and in different groupings.

I was really dragging that afternoon when we walked to an exit and caught a bus back to the university. I had told the students that I had been invited to judge the university's English Club drama contest that evening, so we knew we did not have all the time in the world that afternoon. We did not have to run, but we did walk quickly to a bus stop that seemed miles from where we exited the park. We had visited all three large sections of the park, taken a lot of photos, and bought ears of roasted corn from a stand—a good time was had by all. However, I was glad that we caught a bus at the start of its run and that many of us found seats. This afternoon I was ecstatic to get a seat.

After I had taken a very long shower and put on clean clothes, I walked down my six flights of apartment stairs to wait for the student who was hosting me for the drama contest. Knight was a sophomore and the president of the English Club. She was in charge of everything this evening and was going to take me to dinner before the contest. I saw her rushing toward me. Knight was in the process of setting up stage props for this evening and had left to come and get me. We went to the student dining hall to eat, and after some discussion she did agree to let me pay for at least some of our meal on my food service debit card. She did not really accept the argument that I was not accustomed to having lovely young women buy my dinner. I think this was all right because she had spent all of her money on buying very nice flower vases for each of the judges and various prizes for the participants.

My friends Amber and May from the English Department, one of May's former students, and I were the four judges. Knight voted to break ties, but I am not sure that there were any ties. The students put on acts from six plays. Four of these plays were original; one was a very dark mystery, and another was about two young men coming to CYU as freshmen. Another of the plays was the scene from *The Sound of Music* where the von Trapp children are introduced to Maria. A second American film adaptation was Scarlett's first meeting with Rhett Butler in *Gone with the Wind*. The play about freshmen arriving on campus really stole the show. This play and the male lead in it both got first place. The students in the audience thought that most of the scenes were funny, but the one about the freshmen year was very well done, very funny, and well acted. Similar thoughts must have happened to people in the audience, considering the outbursts of laughter. I think that most American college students could relate to the situations the students acted out.

I was the special guest for the evening and got to draw the names for door prizes, give out awards, and provide comments at the end of the performances. I was very honored to be asked to participate. Although it had been a long day of hiking, sightseeing, and theater critiquing, it had been a tremendous day.

17

Bob's School

Before my wife, Karen, and my daughter Cara came to Beijing to visit, we had talked about where we might go during those nine days. For a while we had discussed going to Xi'an to see the museum that contains the first emperor's terra-cotta army. However, realizing that there were more than nine days of places to see in just Beijing, we decided to see those. We could have spent twenty days just going to places in Beijing. So, although we would have to see Xi'an, Shanghai, and a dozen other cities in China on another visit, we were going to look Beijing over well.

In retrospect I probably tried to cram too many things into these nine days. However, if we had not kept moving, we would not have seen all the wonderful sights. Karen and Cara arrived on Air Canada on a Friday afternoon. Mr. Zhang, the Foreign Affairs director, and I went to pick them up at the airport, and their plane was right on schedule. Everything went very smoothly. Traffic was light, both on the airport tollway and Third Ring Road. The Friday afternoon traffic jams were all in the opposite direction. After settling into the Evergreen Hotel on campus, we walked to my apartment and got ready to meet Frank and Judy for dinner. Judy and Frank ordered dinner at a Korean barbeque restaurant about two miles away from campus. It was a lovely meal, and it gave us time to talk about plans, dreams, and aspirations. Most of the meat (beef, pork, and lamb) we cooked over a grill at the table. In addition, Judy, who is Korean Chinese, ordered some other dishes the restaurant specialized in.

It seems unfair to single out Frank and Judy as two of the nicest young people I could ever have met in China. All of the young people (usually students, and typically at CYU) I met there were extraordinarily nice. Dinner with the two of them was particularly charming that evening.

On Saturday, Lily went with us to the Forbidden City. On Sunday, Emma went with us to Yuanmingyuan and the Summer Palace. After both of these excursions, we went out shopping and then to dinner. It was great not to have to be part of a tour group. To be able to discuss whether we should go one place or another is a luxury tour groups do not get.

On Monday, I decided that just Karen, Cara, and I would take a bold step and go out for the day alone. We took a taxi to the Temple of Heaven. It was a lovely day in May, and the park was very quiet. Cara and I went to the far sides of the circular wall at the Hall of Prayer and could hear each other whispering. The sound traveled around this curved stone wall almost perfectly. We sat on a bench for almost a half hour just admiring the ancient cypress trees. It was such a great place to sit and look and talk that it was difficult to leave and take a taxi to the art market about two dozen blocks away.

At the center of the art market is a 300-year-old brush, paper, and art supply store called Rongbaozhai. This store has the most wonderful selection of things that it really should be a "must see" for any Beijing visitor. Because Cara teaches art, I knew that we had to go there. The second floor of this store is all paintings, some hung on the walls and others available to be looked at on tables. The selection (really a collection) was superb and so extensive that it would have been impossible for me to pick out my favorites. The pictures on the second floor were well beyond our budgets, but it was still fun looking at them as if they were museum pictures. I assume that they were samples of the very best in contemporary Chinese painting. Paintings and watercolors on the first floor were much more modestly priced, and Cara bought one for herself and one for her sister. It was truly difficult to choose one from so many.

Then we went to a barbeque restaurant for a late lunch. This was the first time I had ordered a full meal for myself or others. At the student dining hall or the faculty dining room, I would order one or two dishes and side orders of rice or vegetables. I did get carried away in this restaurant. If I remember correctly, I ordered chicken, beef, lamb, and pork to cook at the table. Our waiter was, thoughtfully, bringing out the platters of meat one at a time and held up bringing the last platter and some other things I may have gone overboard with. We still had so much food that we brought it back to my apartment for a light dinner of leftovers after class.

One of the professors in my class had a son who was five years old. Bob went to a Montessori school that was for the campus of Beijing Institute of Technology. Bob and some of his buddies would say hello to me out in the basketball and exercise area by my apartment building. Cara had told me that she would really like to see an elementary school while she was in Beijing. So I asked Bob's mother whether there was a chance to visit his Montessori school. On Wednesday of that week, Bob and his mother and Cara and I (Karen thought that four adults might be too disruptive) went to the school. What an experience! The school day had begun by the time we arrived. Bob was warmly greeted by his classmates and teachers. The students would get trays from a shelf that had games or toys on them and then they would bring these trays to their mats on the floor to work on.

There was a little girl who said, "Come sit by me, grandfather." I sat on the carpeted floor next to her little mat. She had selected a tray that had a board numbered in tens to one hundred. She wanted a tiny bit of help opening plastic 35mm film canisters that contained ten numbered pieces each. While I sat there, she went from about number twenty to the eighties. She was very careful to place each number on its own space. She never hesitated and was very careful. Bob's class was so cute we hated to move on to the first and second graders. Of course, those children were pretty cute, also, but maybe not quite as cute as Bob's kindergarten class.

On Thursday, Kevin and a driver took us to see the Great Wall at Mutainyu. It was a long drive in one of the university's vans. It seemed to take us twice as long as the bus trip to Badaling's section of the wall. After looking at a map, I saw that it was significantly farther. This section at Mutainyu is very spectacular, with the wall built along a ridge above heavily wooded valleys. There was about a two-mile trail to the top of the mountain ridge, and there was a chairlift available to go up the mountain. Kevin suggested that we all take the chairlift to the top to save time. It was not that hot this day, but it was very humid in the valley, so we did take the lift up to the wall. The view was quite wonderful from there. We could see several miles of wall in both directions. Coming back down from the ridge, we had three options: take the hiking trail back down, take the chairlift down, or ride little cars down on a toboggan-style chute. Karen and I chose to take the chairlift. Our driver, Kevin, and Cara opted for the little cars, the three of them being in their twenties. It should have been an exciting ride down the mountain for the three of them and probably would have been, too, except that an older woman was in a little car just in front of them and rode the brake all the way down the mountain. They were disappointed. It turned out to be a long, slow ride.

We got back to campus that afternoon in time to get cleaned up before I had my American society and culture course. Karen was going to talk with a group of social work and social security majors. My class had about one hundred students less than usual because they had gone to hear Karen talk about her job as our county's child-support officer. The idea of parents not supporting their children sounded very strange to my students, and about two hundred CYU students were interested to hear how the American legal system handled this social problem.

18

Dragon Bone Hill

Zhoukoudian is a very small town about fifty miles south and west of the center of Beijing. The foothills of the mountains come up to the edge of the town. One of these hills had been called Dragon Bone Hill, and in the 1920s a team of Chinese and western scientists found the skullcap of an early ancestor of *Homo sapiens sapiens*. On the day I went to the Peking man site it had been raining for several days off and on. There was a heavy fog over the mountains, and considering that people like us had been visiting or living here for 350,000 years, I thought it seemed like a very magical place. The rain had caused rock and other debris to fall down on the trails. One piece of rock I picked up and looked at had a razor-sharp edge that someone could have easily cut meat with. People had come to this place for the sharp-edged pieces to make hand axes and spear points.

I had driven there with a woman who was in my faculty class and taught Chinese history at CYU. The young man who drove us was the professional driver who had taken us to Mutainyu. Kevin had wanted to go with us today but was needed on campus to show a foreign tour group around the university. The museum and trails at Zhoukoudian were almost completely empty. There were only two foreign tourists at the museum who had taken a taxi from Beijing. When we first arrived, a group of Japanese tourists got off a bus, went to the bathroom, walked around the parking lot, and then got back on their bus. The whole park was ours otherwise, and I remember thinking that it was a shame that Kevin was not also along because the area was so very interesting.

The mountain had a number of pits and caves where fossil remains of animals had been found. One of the pits had a pathway leading downward, and on the side of this small cliff (about seven feet above the path) was a sign indicating that this was where the Peking man skullcap was found. The cliff was made of a mixture of earth and gravel. Evidently, once this fossilized bone was spotted, someone from the team stayed up all night long waiting for rain and dew to loosen it from the earth wall. I could almost imagine how exciting that time must have been for the people involved.

19

Like London?

As I hope is apparent from my description of things in Beijing, my stay there was truly a wonderful experience. Some unexpected things were pleasant surprises, and some other things were just surprises. Take, for example, the Beijing Auto Show. I had no idea that this show would attract the enormous crowds of people that I saw there. Lily and I arrived at the convention center right after the doors opened one Sunday morning. The lines were very long at the ticket windows, so Lily bought our tickets from a scalper for about a third of the regular price. It was not too bad once we got inside the exhibit halls, but before we got inside there were several thousand people being funneled into a small space with only two ticket takers. We saw a wide selection of cars from around the world, including one Rolls Royce and two Bentleys. The newspapers suggested, however, that many people might have been going to the show to see (and perhaps photograph) the young female models instead of the autos. For whatever reason, it was a huge crowd.

In contrast, Emma and I went to see a Chinese production of the British play "Whose Wife Is She Anyway?" Kevin had called the box office on Friday for me, and they indicated that some tickets were still available for Sunday evening. When we got to the theater I bought middle-range tickets (from prices of 100 RMB, 180 RMB, and 250 RMB). Once we got inside we saw that there were only four people inside, and no one else came for ten minutes. Even after the announcement about not taking photos, there was a delay of about twenty minutes before the curtain opened. The theater management must have been waiting to make sure that latecomers bought tickets. There were really only about twenty people in this large theater when the play began. The play was very good, and because it was a farce, I could understand the action well. Emma helped translate the conversations.

This was the first play Emma had ever seen, and she really loved it. The play was funny, and the acting was very good. Evidently there is not yet that much interest in live theater in Beijing. My students wanted to go to see what it was like, but the ticket prices were well beyond their budget. I suggested to them that they should see about getting discount tickets, telling them that I should have bought ones for 100 RMB considering we could have sat anywhere. Several weeks earlier Emma and I had gone to the Beijing Opera's performance of *The Monkey King*. Emma had really liked this as well, but my faculty students were surprised I had even thought of going there. They thought that the opera was boring, but they were in their twenties and thirties (and consider the reaction you would get from Americans in the same age group to Wagner).

Just about everyone in Beijing was anxiously awaiting the middle of June for the World Cup football/soccer matches. This was the first time in forty years that China had qualified. Everyone had an opinion about China's chances, about the strategy of the coach, and about which teams looked the best. On the afternoon that China was playing Turkey or Costa Rica, the newspapers and radio stations reported a major decrease in traffic on Beijing's streets. Most of the matches were shown for CYU students on large screens in two lecture halls. The students packed into the lecture halls and were very enthusiastic. They were also very objective and cheered for all good plays. Watching these matches with the students made me realize what poor sports many American spectators are. The Chinese did not blame the referees for calls, and they did appreciate good plays regardless of who made them. My apartment was packed with students the night that the United States played Korea, and everyone was excited for these two teams because neither was expected to get to the round of sixteen.

Although I did not play any soccer matches or basketball games while I was in China, I did play tennis with Lily and two of her friends (Wang Jing, a roommate, and April, a high school classmate) five or six times. I also went bowling twice with Mr. Zhang and Kevin. The bowling alley was three blocks from the university and had about fifty brand new alleys. The regular bowlers at these lanes were really hoping to have some competition with American bowlers. Perhaps the Brunswick Corporation will set up some competition soon in Beijing. The really good bowlers there are anxious to sharpen their skills and get some tips on improvement. The fact that these beautiful new lanes were there at all certainly surprised me.

I knew that there had been enormous urban redevelopment projects going on in Beijing for the past twenty years. New expressways were built, like Third Ring Road (on which China Youth University was located). However, the extensiveness of the urban renewal efforts did surprise me when Emma, a friend of hers, and I visited an old neighborhood that was being demolished. The homes in this section were probably in the two-hundred- to three-hundred-year-old category. These "homes" were really a walled-in area with three to five buildings inside. Unfortunately, most of these homes did not have water or sewer connections, and many did not have electricity. People frequently did not wish to be moved out of these neighborhoods, either because they wanted their own living space (perhaps even with a little garden) or because they deeply disliked the idea of moving to a high-rise apartment building in the suburbs.

Some workers had been given salvage licenses from the Beijing city government, and we met one of them while we were walking through a market in this old neighborhood. This man had salvaged ten carved stone pieces that had been the doorway to one of these houses. Each of the stone pieces weighed about thirty pounds. So I guess that the entire doorway was more than two hundred pounds. This man offered it to us for 100 RMB. Emma's friend had no place to put it. Emma certainly could not put it in her dormitory room. For $12 U.S. it would have cost hundreds of dollars to ship home—even if I had been able to get an export license for something that old.

My final surprise in Beijing was how difficult it was going to be to leave. I never felt that I wanted to leave—not after eight weeks, not after four months. I knew, though, that I wanted to get home and see my family. My grandson had gone from being a baby to being a little boy, and there was now a granddaughter who I had only seen in photos. I had scheduled my departure from Beijing for July 7. Alvin's second birthday was July 8. It helped me focus on that as my reason for leaving. The last week was hectic. I started grading papers as soon as my last lecture class ended. On a Friday evening and Saturday morning, I graded about seventy final exams. I then worked on the remaining ones in two- and three-hour spurts and finally finished them on Wednesday morning.

Amber and Isabelle from the English Department and I got together to make dumplings for lunch on Monday. They stayed and talked afterward about what teaching was all about and what our expectations were for our students. Each of these young women had just finished master's degrees and was teaching many of the freshmen English classes. It was a great opportunity to see them before I left, make some wonderful dumplings, and find out about their plans for the future.

On Thursday of that week, Kevin and I went to the park outside of Beijing called Fragrant Hills. It is a temple complex with gardens, ponds, and forests. It was an ideal place for us to discuss our future plans (particularly Kevin's) as we walked and talked. Kevin was interested in attending graduate school and had also thought about starting his own business. He is a very capable young man, so I believe that he will be successful in whichever direction he goes. All of the young faculty members and undergraduate students I met at CYU were very capable people. They had all studied hard to get into that university or another university. And, if they were faculty members, then they had to work hard to stay ahead of very bright students. I certainly wish Kevin and the others the best of everything in their endeavors.

Two groups of students I knew I was going to have trouble saying goodbye to were my group of freshmen and the five juniors whom I had gotten to be good friends with. On Saturday morning, the day before I left Beijing, eleven freshmen women, plus one younger brother and one boyfriend, all came to my apartment to make dumplings. I had already done quite a bit of packing and had many other things put away. This was fortunate because that apartment was not built for fourteen people to be moving around and cooking and eating dumplings. The students had brought fillings and dumpling wrappers to make hundreds of dumplings. We made about four hundred dumplings, and I could not imagine our eating all of them for lunch. I was going out to dinner that night and then to breakfast and lunch the next day, so I did not want any leftovers. I should not have worried about this. I think that the one younger brother ate thirty-five dumplings by himself. It did take us a while to cook and eat all of them, but we finished them all off. After that, several students went downstairs to the fruit stand and bought two watermelons, and we had those, too. Rather than being stuck with leftovers, I think that we even managed to clean out other things from my refrigerator.

I was still full from lunch when Alex, Frank, Judy, Emma, their classmate Jimmy (another law student), and I went out to dinner. They also came the next day to help me get my bags downstairs and see me off to the airport. I truly felt as though I was leaving nieces and nephews. I certainly hope that I am not fooling myself by thinking that I will see them all again. They are excellent students who will make wonderful careers for themselves, and I thank them again for making my stay in Beijing an incredible experience.

I have purposely tried not to make this book read like my advice to the traveler. However, if I were to pass along one friendly suggestion to westerners traveling to China, it would be to go to an English corner on Friday night. I believe that you will find people there to meet and talk with who you will never forget. When you return home, you will be telling your friends and relatives about the people you had interesting conversations with this one Friday evening in March or October.

Glossary

Arrow Tower, Bell Tower, Drum Tower. These towers were parts of the defense system for the old city. Beijing had a wall encircling the city at one time, and the Arrow Tower was part of this wall. The Bell Tower and the Drum Tower were located at the north edge of the city to sound alarms at the approach of an enemy army.

Badaling. Badaling, a small tourist village north of Beijing, is the closest and most accessible point on the Great Wall. It is about a ninety-minute trip by tourist bus from the south end of Tian'anmen Square. Regular city buses from the northern terminal take slightly less time for perhaps one-tenth the price. The Chinese tourists are just as excited about going to the Great Wall as westerners.

Behai Park. This park, several blocks north and west of the north entrance to the Palace Museum, is a peaceful lake and recreation area. People find it difficult to imagine that they are in the center of a city of fourteen million people when they are there. Central Park in New York would be a similar experience.

Beijing. The capital of the People's Republic of China, Beijing is situated on the north China plain with mountains to the north and west of the city. It has ancient neighborhoods and modern skyscrapers. It has two modern subway systems, buses of every sort, and the friendliest taxi drivers in the world. Probably only Shanghai and Hong Kong beat shopping here, but Beijing has the old imperial buildings and grounds.

English corner. On Friday evenings in most cities in China, people gather to practice English. The largest "corner" in Beijing is at People's University, about three blocks from the Friendship Hotel. This is a wonderful opportunity to meet and discuss current events, art, architecture, American universities, poetry, literature, and so on with Beijing residents and students from across China.

Hutongs. Hutongs are alleyways in the old neighborhoods that are about wide enough for three bicycles or one small automobile. Urban renewal by the city of Beijing is replacing these sections of the city at a rapid pace. Shops and small restaurants can be found there, but generally these narrow lanes are defined by the outside walls of old homes that became divided into tiny one- or two-room "garden apartments."

Mutainyu. Mutainyu is the second most popular section of the Great Wall visited by tourists. It is about twice as far from Beijing as Badaling. There is a steep climb or chairlift to get to this section of the wall. However, walking along this section is much easier, and the hills at this section are wooded.

Palace Museum (the Forbidden City). One could take several full days to see the magnificent buildings and lovely gardens here. It is one massive museum with displays of gifts, armor, jade, porcelain, and architecture. There are many places to sit and enjoy watching people from every country being tourists.

RMB (Renmibi, People's Money). This money refers to yuan, the highest denomination of currency. One yuan is equal to about twelve U.S. cents. Coins are for fen, mao, and one and two yuan. RMB paper currency is in 1, 2, 5, 10, 50, and 100 yuan notes.

Spring Festival. The Lunar New Year is the largest celebration in China. Most people who are able either return to their hometown or think about visiting family. Trains are packed with persons going "home for the holiday."

Yuanmingyuan (the Old Summer Palace). After being destroyed by western armies in the nineteenth century, this enormous park complex is being rebuilt as a tourist site. Until the 1860s this complex of buildings, lakes, and plantings had been considered one of the loveliest sites on the planet.

Zhoukoudian (the Peking man site). Zhoukoudian is a small mountain where the Peking man remains were found by scientists. The museum there gives a good understanding of the importance of the bones found just several hundred yards away. More unforgettable, however, is to walk on the trails and see the caves that had been used for tens of thousands of years.

About the Author

William Craig counsels prospective students and teaches logic and ethics courses at Governors State University in University Park, Illinois. His undergraduate college advisor deeply loved Asian philosophy and culture and probably would have loved to have visited Bill in Beijing. Bill did go to China without knowing any Chinese except a few words and phrases. He has since taken three classes in Chinese and now knows how much more he has to learn. Bill is a proud father and grandfather, and he and his wife, Karen, live in Rensselaer, Indiana—a much different venue from Beijing.